# The Art of
# Painted Furniture

# The Art of Painted Furniture

## Anita Rosenberg

*There is nothing more homey, cozy, and comfy than painted furniture. Trends and fads may come and go, but history confirms that* The Art of Painted Furniture *is always in vogue.*

Sterling Publishing Co., Inc. New York
A Sterling/Chapelle Book

# Chapelle Ltd.

Owner: Jo Packham

Editor: Linda Orton

Staff: Areta Bingham, Kass Burchett, Jill Dahlberg, Marilyn Goff, Holly Hollingsworth, Susan Jorgensen, Barbara Milburn, Karmen Quinney, Cindy Stoeckl, Kim Taylor, Sara Toliver, Desirée Wybrow

Photography: Dean Alexander
Anita Rosenberg
Rick Szczechowski
David Valenzuela

Library of Congress Cataloging-in-Publication

10 9 8 7 6 5 4 3 2 1

A Sterling/Chapelle Book

Published by Sterling Publishing Company, Inc.
387 Park Avenue South, New York, NY 10016
© 2002 by Anita Rosenberg
Distributed in Canada by Sterling Publishing
℅ Canadian Manda Group, One Atlantic Avenue, Suite 105
Toronto, Ontario, Canada M6K 3E7
Distributed in Great Britain and Europe by Cassell PLC
Wellington House, 125 Strand, London WC2R 0BB, England
Distributed in Australia by Capricorn Link (Australia) Pty Ltd.
P.O. Box 704, Windsor, NSW 2756, Australia
*Printed in China*
*All Rights Reserved*

Sterling ISBN 0-8069-2513-2

If you have any questions or comments, please contact:

Chapelle Ltd., Inc.
P.O. Box 9252
Ogden, UT 84409

Phone: (801) 621-2777
FAX: (801) 621-2788
e-mail: chapelle@chapelleltd.com
website: www.chapelleltd.com

# PREFACE

One of my biggest artistic inspirations comes from the Graffiti art movement of New York City in the late 1970s and early 1980s. Street artists such as Jean-Michel Basquiat, Keith Haring, Futura 2000, Dondi, and Zephyr broke down the artistic barriers of painting only on canvas. They used the entire New York area as their canvas from subway trains to handball courts, walls, storefronts, and everything in between.

One artist from that period, Kenny Scharf, stands out in my mind as the inventor of "customizing." Customizing is a slang term for painting on functional objects such as a toaster, telephone, refrigerator door, and even a Volkswagen® Beetle. Transcending the medium of paint onto useful and workable objects is what we do when we "paint on furniture." Kenny Scharf and his peers are contemporary artists who took customizing everyday objects into art for the masses.

# TABLE OF CONTENTS

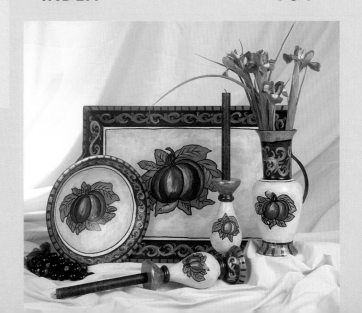

# INTRODUCTION

Painted furniture and accessories are a by-product of days gone by. A simpler life—a more hands-on existence—where time ran slower and furniture created by human hands was a necessity, not a luxury. Your home may be crying out for your personal touch—a meaningful décor item with a history that you can pass on to future generations as something special that came from your soul.

*The Art of Painted Furniture* is a book of inspiration and great ideas. My goal is to encourage and stimulate your imagination while unleashing your artistic talent. I want you to get as excited as I am about painting your own furniture by sharing what inspires me and introducing you to other artists who create masterful works of painted furniture. I want to show you how fun and easy it is to express yourself through your own home décor.

Growing up in Cincinnati, Ohio, I always knew I would be an artist. My mother was creative and my sister and I followed suit. It was not as arrogant as, "Oh, I am going to be an artist," it was more like, "I am a totally visual person and very sensitive (a triple Cancer) and there is so much I need to say and I have no other choice but to say it through art."

My next challenge was to find a medium in which to express myself. While at Walnut Hills High School, I tried many mediums, until one day I discovered welding metal sculpture! Of course, the macho aesthetic involved, appealed to my sense of female liberation at the

time. But more importantly, I discovered that I like to work with "found" objects. I like to find things and assemble them as well as paint them. Some might call this the "Chachka" effect. I prefer to call it an electrifying discovery.

*The Art of Painted Furniture* is an appropriate title for this book. As an artist and filmmaker, my approach to my painted furniture line is as ART. When someone purchases one of my hand-painted tables, lamps, or candlesticks, they now own a piece of my art. It is amazing to me the energy brought into a room by colorful pieces of painted furniture and decorative accessories. My work adds "punch" to the living space.

With this book I would like to share with you not only my work and process, but the work and process of other successful artisans in the field. We will provide you with tips in painting and designing your own furniture. Even if you decide not to paint your own furniture, you will have a new appreciation for the hard work and expertise each and every one of us puts into our creations. Next time you go into a store or gallery that carries hand-painted furniture, you may recognize an artist presented in this book or a painting style we have demonstrated. Enjoy and learn.

**Opposite page:** Mosaic china and painted furniture by Rebecca Dennis and Paula Funt

## chapter 1

# WHAT TO PAINT

So you want to paint and decorate your own furniture. Maybe you are redecorating a room or moving into a new house or apartment. You have seen hand-painted furniture at your local craft gallery or gift store and caught yourself saying, "I can do that!" As an artist and painter of furniture, I encourage you to try your hand. Unleash your artistic talent and create your own masterpiece.

**Left:** Leopard Scroll design detail depicts flowers and leaves
**Opposite page:** Gothic design on stacking tea tables

## TABLES

Tables are the foundation of our furniture selections. Mixing and matching simple utilitarian pieces with colorful hand-painted pieces can bring a smile to your face every time you enter a room.

Tables are fabulously fun to paint. There are so many styles to choose—from simple Shaker pieces to fancy French shapes. Shaker furniture is characterized by its simple lines and tapered legs. The country look has scallops and curvy edges cut into the furniture shape for an added design element. Fancy curved French legs masterfully add a classical dash to the piece.

**Upper left:** Painted stripe and leaf details on butler table
**Upper right:** Crackle technique used in Romantiques design on side table
**Lower left:** Tuscan Farmhouse design on French entry table
**Lower right:** Bamboo and butterfly details on entry table
**Opposite page (upper right):** Versace-inspired scroll design on Shaker table

I primarily paint SMALL OCCASION-AL TABLES. They are functional art pieces that spice up a room.

Tables can also be thought of as having a variety of uses in a room. There are entry tables, side tables, coffee tables, and stacking tea tables, to name a few. Each has a specific use where size and function come into play.

ENTRY TABLES are a good place to begin. The ideal entry table is long and high. They may have drawers and/or bottom shelves. This French entry table (lower right), from my home, has curved legs and a drawer. An entry table, painted with the Bamboo Butterfly design, sports a bottom shelf. It depends on whether you are using the piece for function or drama. These tables look best when simply embellished with a single lamp, a few memorable pieces, and plenty of room for keys, mail, or anything else that you will toss on it when you enter your home.

STACKING TEA TABLES are an "old school" concept, yet I like the idea of bringing them back. They are great to set beside your sofa for functional purposes—to hold snacks and beverages. They can also be cascaded out from the wall as a display piece, such as this set with Red Apple, Blue Grape, and Kacky Pear designs (opposite page). Since they come in sets of three, you can paint them all the same or stir things up by mixing your designs and colors.

Other table shapes include coffee table benches, round tables, square tables, and Cricket tables.

When it comes to coffee tables, I like to challenge convention and paint on benches or large boxes. Coffee table benches work well because they do not take up much room, yet serve the purpose of hosting your remote controls and *TV Guide*. COFFEE TABLE BOXES (right) open up for storage, or several can be grouped together for a unique effect.

ROUND TABLES and SQUARE TABLES are great when cozied up to a reading chair. You can find them with or without a shelf. A small table lamp or standing lamp placed nearby is a must for reading.

Larger tables that make a more dramatic statement include SHAKER TABLES and CRICKET TABLES. Cricket tables are interesting because they have a round top and a triangular bottom shelf. This in itself presents design challenges.

SIDE TABLES can be used to complement your boudoir, or in a hallway or an office. I design side tables with fancy French legs, and BUTLER TABLES with straighter and more simplistic lines. Both have drawers, but only the butler tables have a bottom shelf.

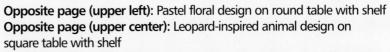
**Opposite page (upper left):** Pastel floral design on round table with shelf
**Opposite page (upper center):** Leopard-inspired animal design on square table with shelf
**Opposite page (upper right):** Bamboo Butterfly design on butler table
**Opposite page (lower left):** Orange Magnolia design on round table
**Upper left:** Contemporary spiral design on cricket table
**Lower left:** African-inspired Leopard Scroll design on side table
**Lower right:** Mosaic and Painted Night Table by Rebecca Dennis and Paula Funt

19

Small painted DINING TABLES, PUB TABLES, DINING CHAIRS, and BAR STOOLS add drama to the kitchen and dining décor. A favorite part of painting my own dining tables is the wild and crazy designs I can create, which make dining a delightful experience.

Mixing chairs and stools around the table creates a most eclectic vibe. It shows great creativity and daring design instincts on your part.

**Opposite page:** Italian-influenced designs mixed and matched on tables, benches, chairs, and stools
**Upper left:** "Jordan's River" round table by Lynn Bonge
**Upper right:** Painted pub table and bar stools

**Left:** Dressing table, mixed media and paint by Elaine Rosenberg
**Upper:** Painted and découpaged side table, lamp, and chest by Robyn Filliman

**Right:** Side tables, painted and découpaged with vintage papers by Tony Mack
**Lower:** "Sanibel" sofa table by Lynn Bonge

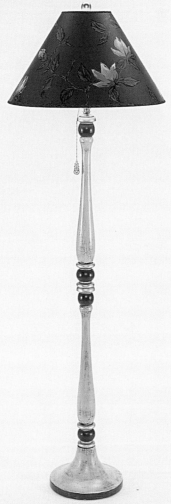

## LAMPS Lighting is so crucial to the ambiance of any environment (think of movies and photography). You will want to maximize your lighting potential and not settle for cheap mass-produced lamps.

Small table lamps are great in pairs, and large table lamps make a statement and give off more light. Standing lamps come in handy just about anywhere. Large lamps look best on larger tables and mantels, whereas smaller lamps are suited for round or side tables. Lights are amazing energy channels. Be creative with your lighting!

Painted shades are extensions of lamps. A painted lamp shade makes the difference as to whether the light shines through the shade or illuminates shafts of light out the bottom and the top of the lamp.

The more paint that you add to the shade, the more the shade becomes the "star!" Adding fringe to the bottom is another style choice, as are drop chains and three-way switches. You can have fun creating inventive finials for the harp. A harp is the metal piece that connects to the light socket and curves up to support the lamp shade. The rule of thumb for selecting harp sizes is that the bottom edge of the shade should come to the top of the lamp without exposing the bulb hardware.

## ACCESSORIES
When it comes to decorating with your painted furniture, no picture would be complete without wonderful accessories. When arranging furniture in my home or in my booth displays at shows, I like to combine shapes. It gives better balance to add a pair of tall candlesticks with a round vase, a bowl, a picture frame, and a lamp. In essence, you are creating a still life. So let your eye scan an arrangement to make certain that it is aesthetically pleasing as well as functional.

original creations by **ANITA ROSENBERG** 5X7

The same techniques used in painted furniture apply to accessories. These become fun, yet functional splashes of design and color.

I began my painting business with PICTURE FRAMES. My first frames (left) were hand-cut with a jigsaw onto which I glued wooden cut-out shapes. A martini glass, the nursery rhyme, *The Cow Jumped Over the Moon,* and tiki statue, were the themes of my early pieces. The Cow Jumped Over the Moon frame was given to Tom Cruise and Nicole Kidman by producer David Geffen as a baby gift.

Other frames that I have designed and made include the Hollywood (upper right) and Ski frames (bottom right), containing my family photographs. The Hollywood frame was derived from an original painting (upper left), inspired by the fact that I live under the Hollywood sign in the Hollywood Hills. The painting was given as a Christmas gift to John Travolta and Kelly Preston by their friend Matt Krane. Other celebrities that own my frames are George Clooney, Jerry Springer, and Jennifer Aniston.

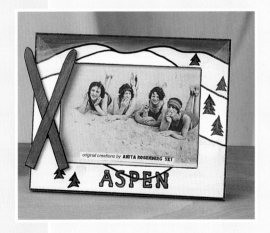

It was my tremendously creative sister Susan who enlarged my repertoire from frames to include wooden CANDLESTICKS. She found unpainted candlesticks at a craft store in Cincinnati, then called and said, "I think you should paint these candlesticks." I did, and the rest is history!

A set of three candlesticks of various sizes is what I call a "Trio." Trios are what I am best known for. I compose 6", 9", and 11"-tall candlesticks into a cluster.

I was invited to appear on the Christopher Lowell Television Show to demonstrate "How to Paint" my famous Gothic-style Trio. The segment was entitled "Enter Laughing." Another one of my favorite trios includes scroll and leaf designs (right).

Additional fabulous painted accessories include mirror frames, SERVING TRAYS, WASTEBASKETS, TISSUE BOXES, CLOCKS, and DECO-RATIVE BOXES.

This is where painting on found objects is really fun as well as a challenge. Stylistic questions to ask yourself are, "Is this a piece to match my room? Is this a gift for someone else? Or, is this an art piece where anything goes?"

We will go into more detail concerning this in Chapters 3 and 4 to help you decide what colors and motifs to use to bring ordinary objects to life.

We cannot forget ceramic accessories. Traditionally, ceramics are glazed and fired in a kiln. Since I am not a ceramicist, I paint them with acrylic paints. I make certain the inside is glazed and waterproof; however, I leave the outside bisque fired, but not glazed. This rough, hard surface absorbs the paint readily and gives a unique look. As long as you use a glossy protective sealer on the outside, the paint will be protected. To my knowledge, no one else is painting on ceramics using this method, and I wanted to share this technique with you.

There is a vast array of ceramic shapes with which to work, such as VASES in all shapes and sizes, PITCHERS, CANISTERS, UMBRELLA STANDS, and PEDESTAL DISHES. The possibilities are endless.

**Opposite page (upper left):** Crackle on extra large vase
**Opposite page (lower left):** Metallic color and details on vase and pedestal dish
**Center:** Metallic paint and wispy technique on canisters
**Lower left:** Bamboo Butterfly design and metallic paints on large vase
**Upper right:** Floral design on umbrella stand, candlesticks, and pitcher

chapter **2**

# WHERE TO FIND YOUR FURNITURE

Now that you have a number of ideas of what to paint, the questions arise, "Where do I find my blanks, i.e. raw, unfinished pieces of furniture, to paint? Or, what if I have an old piece of furniture I no longer like and want to paint over it? How do I do that?" My answer is, "The sky's the limit!" You can paint anything from an old piece you find in your grandmother's attic to an antique you find in a flea market, to a raw, unfinished piece from a wood shop. Here are some places to look.

## FLEA MARKETS, SWAP MEETS, ANTIQUE SHOPS, AND THRIFT STORE FINDS

Flea markets, thrift stores, and yard sales are fantastic sources of inspiration as well as places to locate furniture. There are also antique shops in every town that carry more old and musty things than valuable artifacts. These are my favorite resources. Hitting one of the many Sunday flea markets in Southern California is my passion.

Surrounding myself with an amazing array of vintage and discarded "stuff" gives me so many ideas of new works to create—funky old pieces you can paint over. Every town has its own list of places where there are fabulous bargains waiting to be found by you. There are also weekend yard sales that you probably pass on your way down the street while running errands. Even a trip to your own basement or grandmother's attic may prove to be a gold mine of possibilities.

## UNFINISHED FURNITURE STORES

Unfinished furniture stores are gems. This is where you will find simple pieces, made mostly from pine, that are ready to paint. Some stores even carry paints, stains, brushes, and everything you need to get started. Gather up the supplies you need, then go home and be inventive.

## WOOD SHOP

Some of you might be fortunate enough to have a wood shop of your own. Some may even know a neighbor or relative with a wood shop. My sister Susan and I had such a neighbor and mentor, Al Cornett, who had the most amazing wood shop with a power tool for every job imaginable. Just spending time amidst the sawdust and machinery taught us so much about wood and its many properties.

## chapter 3
# WHAT COLORS TO USE

Now we are getting to the fun part. COLOR choices!

Color is the essence of the painted furniture world. Color is what we live for. It is the color that inspires a piece of art. It is color that breathes life into an ordinary object.

When I am creating a new collection, I first decide whether I want this to have dark warm colors, soft feminine colors, dramatic metallic colors, or bright vibrant colors.

If I am painting a piece for my home, I ask myself, "Which room is this piece going in? Do I want to match a particular fabric or a rug? Am I coordinating my painted piece with the color of the walls? Or, am I going with a style such as Shabby Chic, Exotica, Country Classic, or Cowboy?"

Whatever we decide, color has a dramatic effect on us.

## FENG SHUI AND COLOR

I would like us to begin our color awareness with Feng Shui. The Chinese art of Feng Shui is a good way to study the effects color has on us. Colors create moods, energize, pacify, soothe, and activate. On a recent trip to Hong Kong my tour guide described every building and site in terms of Feng Shui power. She described how important the Chinese consid-ered shapes, color, angles, and that these elements created success or failure for a specific building and its inhabitants. That is why I consider Feng Shui an important influence to include in the color section of this book.

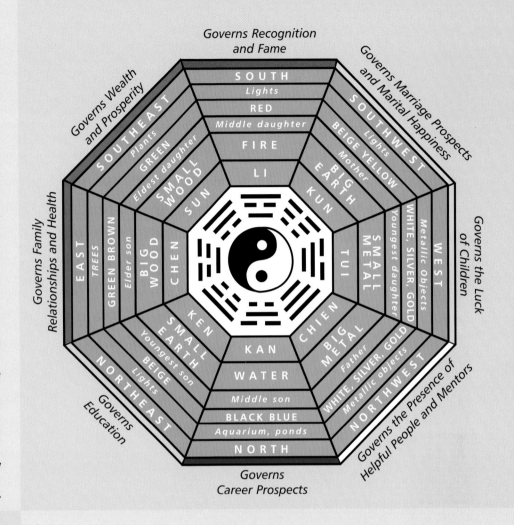

Feng Shui uses a few basic premises when it comes to color. Traditionally, green is for wealth and prosperity. It is also used to promote good health. Purple or red activates the fame area of your house or workplace. Pink attracts love and romance, while blue enhances careers. Earthy brown pro-motes self-knowledge. White, gray, and black are for creativity and travel.

The following is another, albeit looser, interpretation of color:

YELLOW can feel cool if used in a pale tone, or warm if used in a rich tone. I prefer toned-down yellow. It makes me think of keeping myself in good health, of radiant sunshine, and trying to balance all aspects of my life. Yellow used in the kitchen can be healthy and energizing.

RED is fabulously fiery and active, which is difficult to live with in large doses, but energizing when used on side tables, accessories, and lamps. As a rule, too much red in a child's room will never let them have a restful sleep.

PURPLE is a pizzazzy color. It is a great accent color to activate a dull area of your room. Regally speaking, purple possesses the passion of red, which a king must have to make things happen; combined with the calmness of blue, which makes for a wise ruler.

ORANGE is a hot and fun color. On the exotic island of Bali, orange is used as a wondrous accent color on pillows, lamp shades, and fabric covers.

BLUE is a cool calming color that is difficult to work with. I am challenged by blue because it lacks warmth and feels detached. Yet, blue is the color of water and sky, possessing the quality that anything is possible.

## THE BASICS OF COLOR Acrylics

are water-based paints that are easy to use, dry quickly, and clean up with water. Be careful not get them on your clothes, acrylics do not come off from fabrics easily.

    I prefer to use acrylic paint. As an artist who went to art school, I had always used tube paints. That is until my mother and sister introduced me to bottled acrylic craft paints. They come premixed in a vast array of fantastic colors. I have never looked back!

GREEN is really fun to play with. There are so many shades and varieties to choose from. Green is of the earth and represents growth and good health. It can also be used to promote wealth and money. Using green in furniture is bringing the outside inside.

Buying premixed paints skips the fuss. This is the simplest way to achieve desired colors. They can be found in your local art or craft stores. Chain stores carry displays of craft paint. They come in a couple of sizes and all you need to do is pour them into paper or plastic bowls and they are ready for use. The excess paint can be poured back into the bottles to reduce waste.

Mixing your own colors is more of a challenge—the problem is in consistency. Once you mix a color, it is more difficult to go back and recreate that coloration the next time around. The big plus in buying gallons versus ounces of basic colors is cost. You save a lot of money, not to mention all those little bottles that you feel guilty throwing away and not recycling. Buying paint in bulk does not mean they only offer red, yellow, and blue. There are a myriad of fabulous colors to choose from.

PRIMARY COLORS are red, blue, and yellow. These are the colors you use to mix all other colors. Used in their purest forms, these colors are bright and punchy. Children's furniture is often painted in primary colors. For a dramatic and contemporary effect, mix black or white in with red. Adding browns will warm up colors and make them earthier.

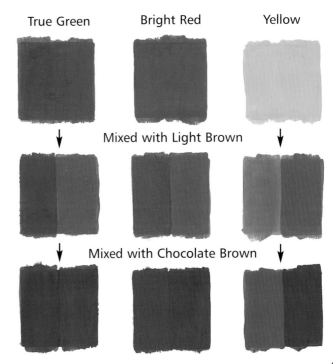

True Green     Bright Red     Yellow

Mixed with Light Brown

Mixed with Chocolate Brown

41

| Emerald | Rose | Sapphire |
|---------|------|----------|
| Brass | Champagne | Red Velvet |

PASTEL COLORS are soft and feminine. Any pastel color can be created by mixing a color with white. White can even be added to a light color to lighten it even more.

For the beach cottage home, lighter fresher colors are preferred. Blues and whites and creams resonate ocean and sea life. Using a whitewash over darker colors can be effective. Using an off-white "wispy" effect as shown in Chapter 5, MY TECHNIQUES is a great way to soften a look.

JEWEL TONES are produced by using metallic-based colors. I describe jewel tones as metallic versions of regular colors such as blue, purple, pink, green, and white. These are different than purely metallic colors, which are named after their metal counterparts: brass, bronze, silver, gold, and copper.

Jewel tones are found in premixed colors. They tend to be transparent, meaning that it paints on thinly and the background can be seen through it. You may want to paint a black base coat underneath, or use two or more coats to reduce the transparency. Exotic Indian and Arabian decorative styles work well with jewel tones.

Mixed with White

Pewter     Copper     Silver

Glorious Gold    Venice Gold    Bronze

Royal Gold    Inca Gold    Russet

**Opposite page:** Detail of design using pastel colors
**Upper:** Metallic paints
**Lower:** Arabian Nights design on bathroom accessories, painted with jewel-tone paints

METALLICS are bold, regal, and dramatic. I love using a dash of metallics in every design I create. It adds "umph!" Metallics are premixed and there are many brands to choose from. What is exciting is that there are so many color variations of metallic colors.

43

## chapter 4

# DISCOVERING THEMES AND MOTIFS

So you have your furniture piece to paint and you have decided what color scheme to work with; you now must decide on a theme or motif for your work.

Motifs and details make or break a piece in my estimation. Nature is where I look for most of my inspiration. I like flowers, vines, leaves, and fruit. There are also animals, insects, abstract shapes, and spiritual symbols. The challenge is to come up with something fresh and new that no one else is doing, or at least put your own unique spin on something you have seen before. This will bring it alive in a whole new way. My favorite reference materials are European magazines, coffee table books, nature walks, museums, fabrics, and trips to exotic locales. See what others are doing and then integrate it into your own vision.

## INSPIRATION FROM TRAVELS

Travels abroad or just down the street can prove to provide a rich source of inspiration. The key is looking at the world with your eyes wide open.

My Grape, Tuscan Farmhouse, and Italy designs were created while traveling throughout Italy. I tried to capture the feeling for the Italian countryside and Chianti region with deep earthy colors such as burgundy, deep purple, olive green, and raw sienna. Themes such as grapes, olives, and worn-and-weathered textured walls of crumbling castles and villas are very inspiring for painting furniture.

The Asian influence has clean simple lines, dynamic colors, hints of nature, and has a spirituality engulfing it. Chinese characters provide excellent icons, as well as bamboo shoots, goldfish, and lily pads.

These accessories (lower), painted with bamboo and butterfly accents, were inspired by a painting (left) I did. I loved the colors and motifs so much, I painted them on furniture and accessories.

Antique Chinese boxes intrigued me after my last trip to mainland China. I am also into spirituality and found the meaning behind the Chinese characters very powerful. I noticed that every Chinese house or establishment had banners with Chinese characters on their door which signified wealth, longevity, love, or happiness. I decided to paint these characters on functional boxes. The surprise is, you must open the boxes to see what fortunes are yours.

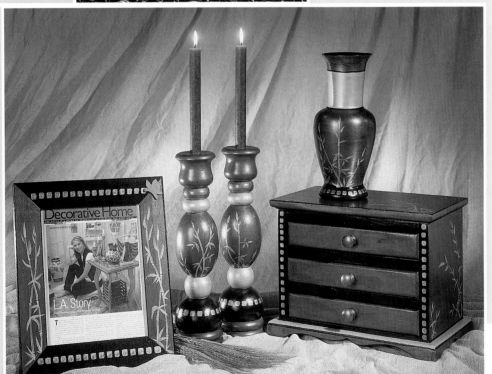

**Upper left and right:** Goldfish design on Chinese boxes
**Lower:** Red Chinese characters on Chinese boxes

**KITSCHY THEMES** There are some themes that are kitschy, based on people's interests or passions. The Golf and Cigar themes were created with that exact purpose in mind. Leafing through books and magazines on your favorite subjects will show you how to best depict your passion onto a piece of furniture.

## INSPIRATION FROM CATALOGUES

A few years ago, Cher came out with a catalogue called *Sanctuary*, which featured her own home décor ideas. I loved the Gothic and Medieval styles in it and, having just started my business, I wanted to create hand-painted furniture that could possibly be introduced through her catalogue. I designed this coloration that was more earthy and country than Gothic, but I called it Gothic style anyway. Although my pieces were never selected for *Sanctuary*, the Gothic design has remained my most popular design ever.

**Left:** Gothic design on table and coordinating accessories

**Left:** Rustic Rose design on vase
**Upper right:** House of Blues design on tray
**Lower right:** House of Blues design on round wire table

## INSPIRATION FROM A CUSTOM JOB

The Rustic Rose design was originally created for the House of Blues in Los Angeles. House of Blues restaurant and nightclub had just opened with a wonderful gift shop featuring original artwork by famous "outsider artists" from all over the South. The folksy worn-and-weathered quality of the House of Blues décor was absolutely my "cup of tea." I created a design that I felt embodied their tone. These pieces were customized with their House of Blues quotes such as, "Help Ever, Hurt Never;" "Unity in Diversity;" and "In Blues We Trust."

The design was so popular with my customers that I still paint it, minus the House of Blues logos and quotes. Sometimes, new styles arrive in the strangest ways.

**Upper left:** Sailboat wall art
**Upper right:** Detail of top of
Nautical design on stacking tea tables
**Lower left:** Lighthouse wall art

## INSPIRATION FROM TRENDS I began

noticing the popularity of the Nautical look emerging at the gift and furniture shows in 1999. Not only were the East Coast seafaring towns of Cape Cod and the Hamptons sporting the styles, but most areas of the country have important bodies of water where the sport of boating was taking a hold on people's decorating ideas.

Maybe it is the concept of bringing your leisure-time activities into your home. Anyway, I saw what others were doing with lighthouses and sailboats, and decided the time had come to do my own take on the theme. That is how the Nautical design came into being.

I wanted to use the Americana colors of red, white, and blue with an antique finish, along with some stars and an anchor on board for good measure.

**Right:** Nautical design on stacking tables, lamp, and candlesticks

## INSPIRATION FROM ANIMAL PRINTS

Exotic animal patterns have always been the rage. As a trend, they come and go with ease every season. Zebra, cheetah, and leopard patterns never seem to die out. Animal prints bring that exotic sense of far-away travel, as well as a sense of fun kitsch. Because of their earthy color schemes, animal fur patterns can mix-and-match with other more brightly colored home décor items.

I like to add a touch of metallic to my animal prints. I think it gives them a sense of royalty and drama.

**Opposite page (upper left):**
Stylistic leopard design detail
**Opposite page (center):**
Sophisticated and detailed leopard
design detail
**Opposite page (upper right):**
Cheetah design detail
**Opposite page (lower):** Leopard
Scroll design detail
**Right:** Leopard design on accessories
**Lower:** Cheetah Safari design on
stacking tea tables

challenge, and a different approach was required for each of the two collections.

Animal patterns are "hot," and over the years I have designed a variety of animal prints. My Leopard spots are sophisticated, with great detail and variations in the background coloration to look like animal hide. The challenge in creating a collection of furniture inspired by the Scotia Design Group's Cheetah Safari was to be different than my previous Leopard designs as well as to add other painterly elements to the mix.

Scotia's Cheetah Safari collection is pattern-on-pattern. Furniture is too busy if pattern-on-pattern is used. What I noticed was a nice earthy quality to this design that I wanted to accentuate.

I liked the green leaves and the Cheetah print best. Minimalizing the Cheetah and maximizing the leaves creates enough of a "jungle safari" look

## A DESIGN PROJECT WITH SCOTIA DESIGN GROUP A project was presented to my studio to work with the rug and pillow designers, Scotia Design Group. My job was to interpret their fabric designs onto coordinating hand-painted furniture. Each design presented a different and unique

without beating you over the head. Since black is the fringe color on the pillows and rugs, I wanted to use black as an edge color on the furniture in the same way. And then there's this terrific red accent I thought would look great in my worn-and-weathered effect as demonstrated in Chapter 5, MY TECHNIQUES. I then added a cream-colored worn-and-weathered effect to make the furniture look aged (left).

The Tuscan Farmhouse design (page 14) is one of my favorite designs. It utilizes the great colors with which people love to decorate their homes—burgundy, plum, green, and sienna. I painted the colors in a striped pattern over a black base coat. I wanted to adapt this design for Scotia Design's Balmoral collection.

The Balmoral collection (right) is complex, with many colors and patterns. The elements I picked up on were the color green and the paisley details. The lamp base was painted a worn-and-weathered green. The lamp shade was painted similar to the Tuscan Farmhouse lamp shade.

Once the base coats were in place, the paisley details were added. The gold accents were painted last, making the lamp look exotic. A bejeweled touch adds a rich and fabulous element.

## chapter 5
# MY TECHNIQUES

Now, you have ideas and information on how to select furniture, where to find it, what to focus on, and how to select motifs. Let's get started and paint furniture!

The Gothic design on a butler table (left) utilizes several of my "famous" techniques such as wispy, stain, swirl, detail, and wood cutouts. I think its popularity comes from the versatile color combination of blue, green, gold, and copper. The design is both masculine and feminine. And the butler table itself has a drawer and bottom shelf which allows for many home décor uses.

# How-To Paint the Gothic Design on a Butler Table

## Materials & Supplies for Step 1

Palm sander (optional)
Pine butler table: unpainted
Putty knife: 1"
Sandpaper: 100 grit
Spray primer or sealer
Wood putty: neutral

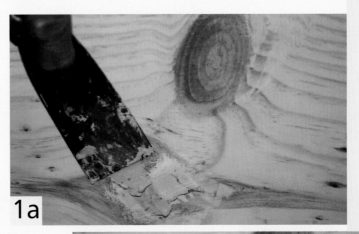
1a

## 1 PRIME & SEAL

*Begin with an unpainted, or "blank," pine butler table. Most pine furniture blanks have knots and imperfections. The knots must be sealed and primed so they will not bleed sap or turn brown as the wood ages.*

Apply wood putty over any surface imperfections and holes in knots, using putty knife. Smooth out putty and allow to dry.

Sand wood putty, using sandpaper and/or palm sander.

Spray primer over knots and puttied areas. Allow to dry.

1b

1c

## SELECTING A BRUSH

Your choice of brush is very important. Prices of paintbrushes range from $2.00 to $100.00. Of course, I prefer the more expensive ones because they have natural fiber bristles and give the smoothest strokes. It is important to feel the brush against your hand to see if it is too stiff, too soft, too artificial, too short, or just right.

A variety of paintbrushes for different effects is crucial. If you are painting large surfaces, you will want brushes ranging from 2" to 4" in width. For detail work, you will want fine-point brushes in sizes 0–00. There are paintbrushes with slanted edges and flat edges, as well as brushes with rounded tips.

## 2 BASE COAT

2a

*When it comes to paint, I have a preference for acrylic paints. Acrylics are water-based paints which are easy to use, and dry quickly. They clean up with water and come in many premixed colors.*

**Materials & Supplies for Step 2**

Acrylic paints: blue; green
Paintbrush: 1" flat
Plastic bowls (2)
Glass jar and water

2b

Squeeze blue paint into a bowl. Apply paint as smoothly and neatly as possible onto tabletop and legs. Allow to dry.

Squeeze green paint into remaining bowl and apply paint as smoothly and neatly as possible onto inside and outside of drawer and bottom shelf. Allow to dry.

2c

## Materials & Supplies for Step 3

Acrylic paint: off-white
Paintbrush: #9 or #11 round,
    very soft
Plastic bowl
Glass jar and water

3a

3b

## 3 WISPY

*One of my "famous" techniques is WISPY. The name came into being because it describes the way the paintbrush is used. The wispy effect is done with a soft inexpensive brush, "wisping" one color on top of another. This is done with either a light color over a dark color or vice versa. For the Gothic design, I use an off-white wispy because it gives an antique look.*

Squeeze paint into bowl. Daub paintbrush into paint and wipe off excess paint on edge of bowl. Using quick, rapid strokes, wisp the paint over the blue and green base coats. You will want it to look messy and random, with the paint clumpy in some spots and thin in others. Wisp paint over all blue and green painted surfaces. Allow to dry.

## Materials & Supplies for Step 4

Paintbrush: 1" flat, stiff
Plastic bowl
Stain: lt. oak
Sponge: soft, smooth

## 4 STAIN

*Since the layering of paint is my favorite technique, we will add a light oak stain over the wispy surfaces. This gives added depth and a sense of aging to the piece. A soft sponge can be wiped over the surfaces, or a stiff brush may be used to scrub in the stain.*

Pour stain into bowl. Apply stain onto sponge, using paintbrush.

Wipe stain evenly over the painted surfaces. Do not allow stain to concentrate in one area. Allow to dry.

4a

4b

4c

**GOTHIC WISPY**

Lt. Oak Stain

Lt. Oak Stain over
Gothic Wispy

5a

5b

5c

# 5 METALLIC BASE COATS

*Metallic paints tend to be translucent and may require two coats for the surface to look thick and solid.*

Squeeze copper paint into a bowl. Apply paint as smoothly and neatly as possible onto front and sides of table. Allow to dry.

Squeeze gold paint into remaining bowl and apply paint as smoothly and neatly as possible onto top trim edge of table. Allow to dry.

## Materials & Supplies for Step 6

Acrylic paints: black; metallic copper; metallic gold
Paint marker: black, fine-line
Paintbrushes: #1 round; #2 round
Plastic bowls (3)

## 6 PAINTED DETAILS

*Details, swirls, and leaves can now be added to your painted furniture.*

### SWIRLS
Squeeze black paint into a bowl. Paint ½"–⅝" dots around outside edge of green shelf, using #2 paintbrush. Allow to dry.

Squeeze copper paint into a bowl. Paint swirls onto black dots, using a #1 paintbrush. Allow to dry.

### LEAVES
Squeeze gold paint into remaining bowl. Paint small leaf shapes around inside edge of tabletop, using #2 paintbrush. Allow to dry.

Draw leaf veins onto gold leaf shapes, using fine-line paint marker. Allow to dry.

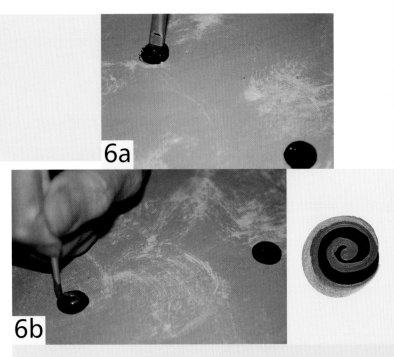

6a

6b

6c

6d

## Additional Materials & Supplies for Step 6

Paint markers: black, broad-line;
gold, medium-line

*Paint markers are one of the best inventions I can think of. Originally, I got "turned onto" them during my graffiti days in New York City. Always remember to shake paint markers before using them. Old school masters like Zephyr, Dondi, Futura 2000, and Fab 5 Freddy taught me that paint markers will write on any surface.*

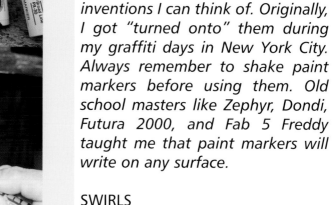

6e

### SWIRLS
Paint random swirls on decorative table edge, using gold marker. Allow to dry.

### OUTLINING
Outline table edges, using black marker. Allow to dry.

6f

In the early '80s there was not a graffiti artist who did not "tag" (write their name) around New York City with a paint marker. These were "arty" signatures and messages to one another, unlike gang-related scribbles. It was a major art movement of "burners" on subway trains and murals on handball courts. This opened the doors for Graffiti artists—Jean-Michel Basquiat, Kenny Scharf, and Keith Haring—to make their way into major galleries and museums.

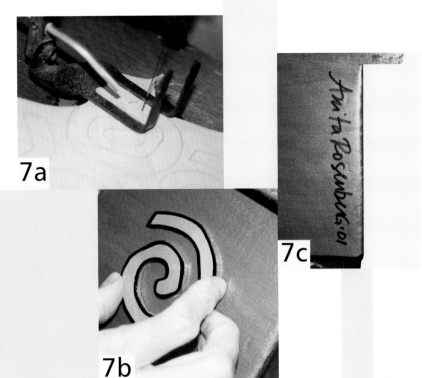

**7a**

**7b**

**7c**

**Materials & Supplies for Step 7**

Luan wood: ¼" thick
Mallet: soft head
Metal studs
Metallic paints: copper; gold
Paint marker: black, medium-line
Paintbrush: ½" flat
Pencil
Permanent marker: black, fine-line
Plastic bowls: (2)
Sandpaper: 100 grit
Screwdriver
Scroll saw: fine blade
Tassel: 3" long
Wooden drawer pull
Yellow wood glue

**7    THE FINAL DETAILS**

*Wooden cut-out shapes, studs, and tassels are optional. It is, however, mandatory that you sign and date each piece. A permanent marker works well for this.*

WOODEN CUTOUTS
Draw two small and two large swirl patterns onto wood, using pencil. Cut out swirl shapes, using scroll saw. Sand edges of cutouts.

Squeeze gold paint into bowl. Paint large cutouts. Allow to dry.

Squeeze copper paint into remaining bowl. Paint drawer pull and small cutouts. Allow to dry.

Outline edges of cutouts, using black paint marker. Allow to dry.

Apply glue onto backs of small cutouts and place onto back of top decorative edge as shown in photograph on page 58.

Apply glue onto backs of large cutouts and place on front of table as shown in photograph on page 58.

METAL STUDS
Hammer metal studs along top of decorative edge.

SIGNATURE
Sign and date furniture piece, using permanent marker.

DRAWER PULL
Attach drawer pull, then loop tassel over pull.

## Materials & Supplies for Step 8

Gloss sealer: clear finish
Paintbrush: inexpensive 1½" flat

8a

# 8 PROTECTIVE FINISH

*Glazes or gloss sealers are important to protect the surface of your furniture. I only use sealers that dry clear with no yellow residue. Your local hardware or home improvement store will carry an assortment of clear coats in many brands. Try to purchase one that is water- or acrylic-based, making certain that it does not yellow. Ask a hardware store employee for assistance if you are uncertain. Apply 2–3 coats for protection.*

Apply sealer over entire surface of table. Allow to dry between applications.

**CLEANUP** You have completed your project and will want to clean up and take care of those expensive brushes as soon as possible so that they will last a very long time.

Since acrylic paints are plastic, they dry quickly and will make your bristles stiff. If paintbrushes are not thoroughly cleaned, the paint will harden in the bristles, giving the paintbrush less movability, until it eventually becomes stiff.

Other products on the market clean paintbrushes well, but I find that a bar of soap works just fine. Keep paintbrushes in a container of water until cleanup time. This keeps the bristles wet until they can be cleaned. Scrub the paintbrush on the soap and work the soap into the bristles with your fingers. Do not press so hard as to ruin the bristles, but press hard enough to remove all of the paint.

**METALLIC WISPY**

| Wicker | Off-white | Wispy | Lt. Oak Stain | Wispy with Stain |
|---|---|---|---|---|
| Black | Lt. Peach | Wispy | Lt. Oak Stain | Wispy with Stain |

**WISPY** Wispy is the effect of "wisping" one color onto another with a soft brush as demonstrated in How-To Paint the Gothic Design on a Butler Table in Step 3 on page 62. The following will illustrate how great this effect looks when using other colors.

In the METALLIC design I use two different wispy looks. One is light and the other is dark. The light effect is achieved with an off-white wispy applied over a wicker color, which is then completed with a light oak stain. Light peach-colored wispy is applied over black and then stained with light oak, creating a darker look.

COUNTRY CHIC has a "shabby chic" look with soft-colored wispies. This collection mixes and match-es well with romantic modern pieces, funky antiques, and collectibles from your grandmother's attic. The light-colored wispy base coat sets the stage for the pink roses and Versace-like metallic details.

For the darker coloration, begin with a wicker color for the base, then wispy soft white over it. For the lighter coloration, use linen for the base color, and wispy soft white over it.

## COUNTRY CHIC WISPY

Wicker

Wispy with
Soft White

Linen

Wispy with
Soft White

The GRAPE design was inspired by a trip to Italy as well as my love of "kitchen art." I adore anything that goes into making the kitchen a fun and festive place to be.

Wispies begin with an antique white base and a creamy gold wisped on top. This is the case of a darker color on top of a lighter one. The second wispy I like to use is a red over burgundy. These colors are close in hue and when added together, give depth to the coloration.

## GRAPE WISPY

| Burgundy | Rustic Red | Wispy |
| --- | --- | --- |

| Antique White | Tumbleweed | Wispy |
| --- | --- | --- |

**STROKEY** It takes three layers to achieve the strokey effect. The NAUTICAL designs utilize the strokey effect. Begin with a base coat of dark blue, red oxide, or antique white. Next, take a stiff-bristled paintbrush and create long, quick, straight strokes with your second color of soldier blue over dark blue, raw umber over red oxide, or wicker over antique white. The strokes can be painted in different directions, depending on how you like it. The third coat is used as an accent. It gives the illusion of splashes of color. These strokes should be done with a dry brush and are very light. Top colors include soft white or linen.

The use of the strokey technique on these Nautical designs makes the furnishings look like they have been either beached on the sandy shores or weathered by the sea salt air.

## NAUTICAL STROKEY

Dk. Blue

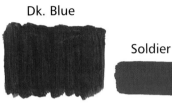

Soldier Blue

Strokey

Strokey with Soft White

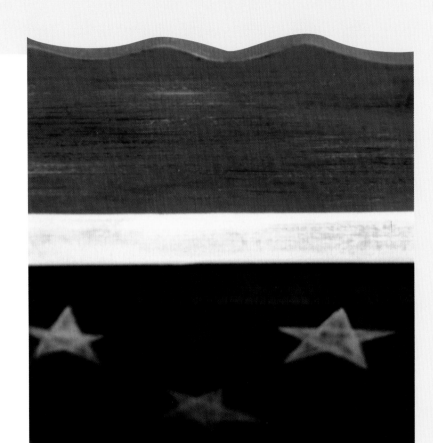

Red Oxide

Strokey

Strokey with Linen

Raw Umber

Antique White

Strokey

Wicker

## WORN AND WEATHERED

The worn-and-weathered look creates an antique look with paint. Achieving multilayer aging with the use of multiple colors and paint strokes rather than sanding off paint layers is more fun as well as allowing for more control.

**Left:** Rustic design on stacking tables and ceramic jars

## How-To Paint the Rustic Design on a Canister Set

**Materials & Supplies for Step 1**

Acrylic paints: chocolate brown,
  dk. reddish brown, raw umber
Ceramic canister set: glazed and fired
  on inside, bisque finish on outside
Paintbrush: 1" flat
Plastic bowls (3)

**1** BASE COAT

*Determine color of each canister section. Dark reddish brown is the base coat for rustic yellow, chocolate brown is the base coat for rustic white, and raw umber is the base coat for rustic green.*

Squeeze each paint into separate bowls. Apply paint as smoothly and neatly as possible onto canister sections as desired. Allow to dry.

## RUSTIC WHITE

**Chocolate Brown**

**Linen**

**Antique White
Lt. Oak Stain**

## RUSTIC YELLOW

**Dk. Reddish Brown**

**Yellow Gold**

**Antique White
Red Oxide**

## RUSTIC GREEN

**Raw Umber**

**Olive Green**

**Lt. Green**

## Materials & Supplies for Step 2

Acrylic paints: yellow gold, olive green, linen
Paintbrush: 1½" flat, long stiff bristles
Plastic bowls (3)

## 2  ADDING A SECOND COLOR

Squeeze each paint into separate bowls. Apply second color with quick horizontal and vertical strokes over base coats. Make certain that some base color still shows through. Note: Keep brush dry so that strokes remain rustic-looking from beginning to end. Allow to dry.

Olive Green over Raw Umber

**2a**

Lt. Green over Olive Green

## Materials & Supplies for Step 3

Acrylic paints: lt. green, red oxide,
   antique white
Stain: lt. oak
Paintbrush: 1½" flat, long stiff bristles
Plastic bowls (4)

White over Yellow Gold

## 3   BRUSHING ON FINAL COLOR

*The point of this step is to give the canisters a final rustic look as if they have been in an old barn or on a dusty shelf in an antique store.*

Squeeze each paint and each stain into separate bowls. Apply accent colors over first and second paint layers, using a dry paintbrush. Allow to dry.

Details may be added. See How-To Paint the Gothic Butler Table, Step 6 on page 66 for ideas.

Lt. Oak Stain over Antique White

**LAYERING** Layering colors on top of other colors gives a dramatic effect. In the Tuscan Farmhouse design, I use black as the base coat. When more vibrant colors are painted on top, such as a brick red, olive green, plum, and dark gold, they take on a richer and deeper hue. If you use a large brush and your strokes are straight and slightly sloppy, leaving some of the black showing, you end up with a layered effect.

## Brick Red over Black

## Olive Green over Black

## Raw Sienna over Black

## Plum over Black

### Leaf Detail

### Swirl Detail

**Base Coats**

Metallic paints are great to layer over solid colors or even other metallics as shown on this serving tray (left) and side table (lower). Since they have a translucent quality, you can achieve a variety of effects, depending on which colors go over or under other colors. Using metallics gives an elegant and expensive look.

**Copper over Black**

**Gold over Black**

**Antique Silver over Copper**

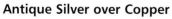

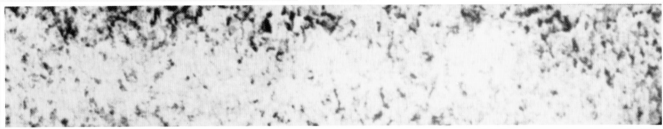

## SPONGING

SPONGING  Sponging is another multilayer effect that can add the elements of a worn, weathered, and antique finish to your furniture. Sponges create texture, and I enjoy using the sponge effect with metallic colors. A natural ocean sponge works best because it has larger and more irregular holes, giving a natural pattern.

**Brass over Black**

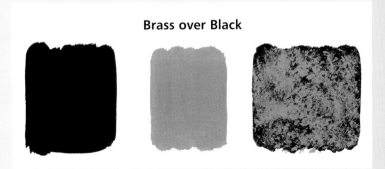

To create the sponged effect shown on this large vase (lower left), you will first need to base coat the piece with a solid color such as black. Moisten the sponge with water and daub into paint. Daub off excess paint on the edge of the bowl. Pat the sponge loosely over the base coat. Repetition determines how tight or loose the sponged effect is—the more times that the sponge is patted over an area, the tighter the finished effect and vice versa.

**Gold over Copper**

The Italian-influenced design on this butler table (right) is an example of sponged copper over gold.

The sponged area of the Orange Magnolia design on the accessories (lower) is bronze over rust red.

**Bronze over Rust Red**

**CRACKLE** Crackle is a complex effect and different crackle products make different sized crackles. I suggest you try various brands of crackle medium to compare the size of crackles. Experiment and you might invent your own effect.

A base coat is painted on the furniture and allowed to dry. The crackle medium is then applied over the base coat with an inexpensive, stiff-bristled brush and allowed to dry. A thick top coat is then applied over the crackle medium. As the paint dries, the crackle will begin to appear, following the direction of the brush strokes. The crackles begin immediately, so if you try to go over the same area a second time, the effect will be ruined.

The Romantiques design includes two colors of wispy paint applied over the dried surface with a soft brush to add complexity and texture. A glaze is then applied over the top of the painted surface to protect it.

### ROMANTIQUES CRACKLE

| Brown Umber | Honey | Crackle Effect |
| --- | --- | --- |

Romantiques Wispy Colors: Lt. Green and Mushroom

**Opposite page:** Detail of Romantiques design crackle
**Right:** Crackle technique on coordinating furniture and accessories

85

The Black and White Toile design (opposite page) is totally crackle. I wanted to create a warm and neutral coloration, using an off-white top coat with minimal detail. This is a design that mixes and matches well with any home décor. It is an extremely simple process where raw umber paint is applied as the base coat with a linen color painted over the crackle medium. A gloss sealer to protect the finish completes the process.

The crackle effect is also used on the ceramic hen and rooster (upper). The aged effect is achieved by staining them, but adding small patches of crackle amazingly ages them more.

An off-white base coat is applied to the bisque ceramics and allowed to dry. An antiquing glaze is wiped over the ceramics with a soft sponge and allowed to dry. Crackle medium is then added in random patches. After the crackle medium has dried, the glaze is again applied over

**BLACK AND WHITE TOILE CRACKLE**

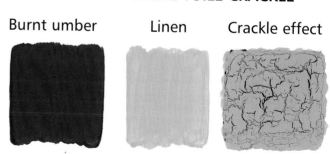

| Burnt umber | Linen | Crackle effect |
| --- | --- | --- |

the patches, and crackles appear more prominent. Additional glaze is applied over crackle spots and allowed to dry. Protect the ceramics with a top coat of glaze.

**DETAILS** Details can make-or-break your piece. Detail gives a focal point. Throughout history, various furniture makers were known for their trademark details.

In the vase design (right), I use a Versace-like gold scroll detail, which is one of the hall-marks of the Italy design.

**VERSACE-INSPIRED SCROLL DETAIL**

On the stacking tables (upper), I combine gold swirls and leaves for the Tuscan Farmhouse design as shown in the detail (right).

Icons and images are what the eye focuses on. PLANTS and FLORALS are some of my favorite images to paint.

# How-To Paint the Leopard Scroll Design on a Vase

**Materials & Supplies for Step 1**

Acrylic paints: black; off-white
Ceramic vase: Glazed and fired
    on inside, bisque finish on outside
Paintbrushes: 1" flat; #2 round
Pencil
Plastic bowls (2)

## 1 BASE COAT

*A medium-sized vase with a large rounded bottom was used for this project.*

Squeeze black paint into a bowl. Apply paint as smoothly and neatly as possible onto lower rounded section of vase, using flat paintbrush. Allow to dry.

Squeeze off-white paint into remaining bowl. Apply paint as smoothly and neatly as possible onto upper neck section of vase. Allow to dry.

Draw zebra stripes onto neck of vase, using pencil. Paint stripes with black paint, using round paintbrush.

**Materials & Supplies for Step 2**

Acrylic paints: honey; tumbleweed
Paintbrush: #2 round
Pencil
Plastic bowl

## BEGINNING LEAVES

Draw leaves onto vase, using pencil.

Squeeze tumbleweed paint into one side of bowl. Paint leaves, filling in outlines. Allow to dry.

Squeeze honey paint into clean side of bowl. Highlight edges of leaves. Allow to dry.

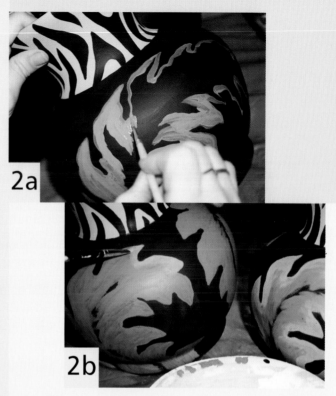

**Materials & Supplies for Step 3**

Acrylic paint: lt. mauve
Paintbrush: #2 round
Pencil
Plastic bowls

## 3 FLOWER PETALS

Draw flower petals onto vase, using pencil.

Squeeze paint into one side of bowl. Paint flowers, filling in outlines. Allow to dry. Cover bowl and set aside excess paint.

**Materials & Supplies for Step 4**

Acrylic paint: pine green
Paintbrush: #2 round
Pencil
Plastic bowl

4a

## 4 FLOWER LEAVES

Draw flower leaves onto vase, using pencil.

Squeeze paint into one side of bowl. Paint leaves, filling in outlines. Allow to dry. Cover bowl and set aside excess paint.

**Materials & Supplies for Step 5**

Acrylic paints: lt. green; pink
Excess paint from Steps 3 & 4
Gloss sealer: clear
Paintbrushes: 1" flat; #2 round

## 5 FLOWER PETAL & LEAF DETAILS

Squeeze pink paint into bowl containing mauve paint. Paint details onto flowers, using round paintbrush. Allow to dry.

Squeeze lt. green paint into bowl containing pine green paint. Paint details onto flower leaves. Allow to dry.

Apply gloss sealer to outside of vase, using flat paintbrush.

5a

FRUITS and vegetables are perfect for kitchens and dining rooms. I created the following fruit designs as seen in the Kacky Pear (upper left), '50s Fruit (lower left), Red Grapes (upper right), and Grape Leaf (lower right) details.

Grapes are a lot of fun to paint and I like to use tone-on-tone when creating them. These photos illustrate the steps I take when creating the grapes. I begin by sketching the grapes and leaves onto the furniture or accessory.

Barn red, off-white, and white acrylic paints are used to create the grapes in the illustration. The grapes and leaves are filled in with barn red paint. A small amount of white is mixed into the barn red paint to create a lighter version of barn red. The paint blend is used to paint the circles of the grapes and fill in the leaves, leaving the vines dark. Barn red is then mixed with off-white, creating a still lighter hue of barn red. Another layer is painted onto the grapes and leaves as a highlighting effect. Highlight stripes are painted onto the grapes as the final and finishing step.

**Upper left:** Detail of Blue Grape design

**Lower left:** Detail of Green Grape design

**Upper right:** Detail of Red Grape design

**Lower right:** Red Grape design on mirror frame

Country and barnyard ANIMALS are popular. The "toile" technique of tone-on-tone is used for the rooster, swan, cow, and horse.

**Upper left:** Detail of Rooster design
**Lower left:** Detail of Swan design
**Upper right:** Rooster design on serving tray
**Lower right:** Swan design on side table

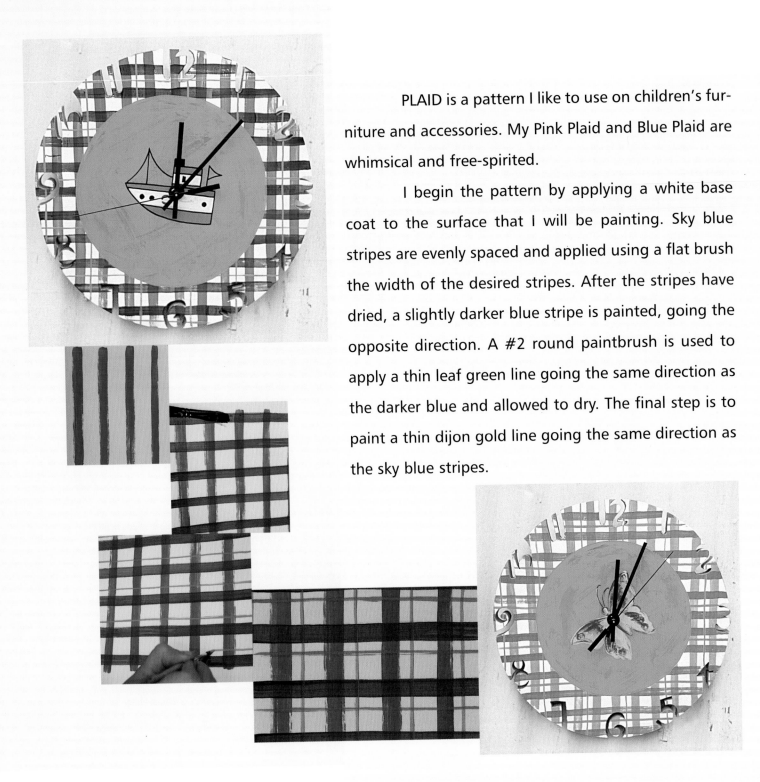

PLAID is a pattern I like to use on children's furniture and accessories. My Pink Plaid and Blue Plaid are whimsical and free-spirited.

I begin the pattern by applying a white base coat to the surface that I will be painting. Sky blue stripes are evenly spaced and applied using a flat brush the width of the desired stripes. After the stripes have dried, a slightly darker blue stripe is painted, going the opposite direction. A #2 round paintbrush is used to apply a thin leaf green line going the same direction as the darker blue and allowed to dry. The final step is to paint a thin dijon gold line going the same direction as the sky blue stripes.

Although LAMP SHADES are not a technique, they require a different approach than wood and ceramic.

I paint on paper lamp shades, or more specifically, parchment. The appearance of the lamp shades is one way when the light is off and another when the light is on. Light shines through the lamp shade and you can see every paint stroke, which does not allow for any margin of error. Some designs such as, French Country (upper), and French Chic (upper center) are soft and romantic and work well on lamp shades.

A more recent design element I like is to paint over a black opaque shade. The light shines out from the top and bottom of the lamp shade. Designs painted like this are bolder and more daring. The lamp base can be painted in a simple pattern with less detail because the more elaborate design work is saved for the lamp shade. Some styles, such as the Tuscan Farmhouse (lower center) and Romantique (lower) designs, work well for painting the shade design in multiple layers.

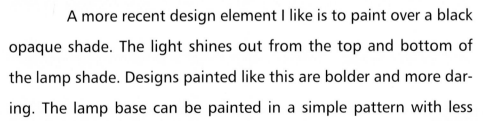

## chapter 6
# GUEST ARTISTS

A book on *The Art of Painted Furniture* would not be complete without inviting guest artists to participate and share some of their secrets with you. Since embarking on my journey into the creative world of home décor and furnishings, I have been privileged to meet and learn from some of the most fascinating artisans in their fields. Allow me to introduce them to you.

**Center:** Rebecca Dennis and Paula Funt are a dynamic sister team whose bold and colorful mosaic furniture is unsurpassed in originality and technique.

**Upper:** Lynn Bonge is a true original whose elegant and sophisticated style of painting on furniture rivals any European master.

**Lower:** Robyn Filliman is a fine artist with an original and fanciful technique for découpaging color copies of her paintings onto furniture for a fascinating effect.

**Upper:** Susan Wechsler is my sister and a source of inspiration, whose passionate and energetic style dances onto every piece she creates through her amazing imagination.

**Lower left:** Elaine Rosenberg is my mother, mentor, and talented artist whose complex use of mixing mediums makes her painted furniture revolutionary.

**Lower right:** Tony Mack is an imaginative artist of the highest caliber, whose elaborate techniques for artful furniture encompass everything from Picassiette to découpage.

**REBECCA DENNIS AND PAULA FUNT** Rebecca and Paula are the design principals and creators of Mosaicwares, a company founded on the ancient technique of mosaics. Functional pieces are important to them and each of their creations integrates their creative spirit.

As sisters, they have always found working together natural and comfortable. They come from a close-knit family with European roots tied to the arts.

Paula completed her degree in Interior Design at the Ryerson Polytechnical Institute in Toronto, and Rebecca attended the University of Waterloo in Waterloo, Ontario, in Kinesiology, spending as much time as possible in the Art Department. With these credentials, they began working in the family business, a lumber and home center. Their father had hoped that his only son would eventually take over the business, but instead, his three daughters helped run it. It was in the family business that Rebecca and Paula gained their knowledge concerning raw materials, hardware components, adhesives, and machinery; and with this, their world of business evolved.

Vintage china mosaics, beading, fabrics, and wrought iron and wood frameworks were added to their product line satisfying their love of the color, pattern, and texture in antiques and interiors.

**Opposite page (left):** Queen Anne's Lamp, lamp base is covered with vintage china mosaic patterns
**Opposite page (right):** Crown Jewel Box, made from vintage mosaics and crowned with a hand-painted finial
**Lower:** Phoenix Cabinet, cameos of mosaic patterns across the front and hand-made ceramic knobs
**Right:** Detail of Manhattan Cabinet, functional entertainment center with blocks of mosaic patterns on a solid wood frame

# MOSAIC AND PAINTED NIGHT TABLE

## Materials & Supplies

Cardboard templates*
Ceramic tiles (optional)
Disposable plastic container
Drawer knobs (2)
Dust mask
Floor grout: pearl white
Latex ceramic adhesive
Latex paint primer
Latex paints: ivory; 3 assorted
    colors
Masking tape
Night table: prepped**
Packaging paper
Paintbrushes: ¾" flat; 2" flat;
    #5 round, stiff
Permanent marker: black
Rubber gloves
Safety glasses
Sealer: clear, gloss, or satin
Sponge
Straightedge
Tile cutting board or glass cutter
Tile nipper
Unnotched trowel: 1½"
Vintage china dishes
Wood: flat
Water

*Draw design elements such as
swirls onto cardboard and cut out
for templates.
**Prepped as applicable. See
page 57.

**2**

**1** Paint primer onto night table, using 2" flat paintbrush. Allow to dry.

**2** Sketch pattern onto night table as desired, using templates and marker.

**3** Wearing safety glasses and rubber gloves, practice clipping china into ½"–1" triangular-shaped shards from extra dishes, using tile nipper. Note: You will have more control over the cut shape if only half of nipper blade is on the shard. Shapes can be easily cut out by slowly nibbling away at the shards.

**4** Spread ceramic adhesive ⅛" thick over a 3" area of tabletop, using trowel. Note: Design is started in center, then side edges must be done before top outside edges.

**5** Clip china into ½"–1" triangular-shaped shards for tabletop. Score squares or rectangles for table edges, using tile cutting board. Note: Use straightedge if using glass cutter.

**6** Place cut shards into adhesive, following the design and keeping pieces as close as possible. Make certain to leave space for drawer knobs. Note: Since china shards may vary in thickness, allow thinner pieces to float on adhesive.

**7** Once a section is set with shards, lay wood across shards, making certain that wood rests on two thicker pieces. Gently press shards down simultaneously to keep an overall evenness. Allow adhesive to dry 24 hours.

**8** Mix grout 4:1 with water in container. Mix well until mixture is consistency of paste. Notes: Always add water to grout powder, wearing dust mask. Consistency may be adjusted by adding additional water or grout.

**9** Using gloved fingers, spread grout over surface and massage grout across shards in all directions to ease grout between spaces. Wipe off excess grout before it dries, using damp sponge. Note: Grout hardens quickly and becomes impossible to remove.

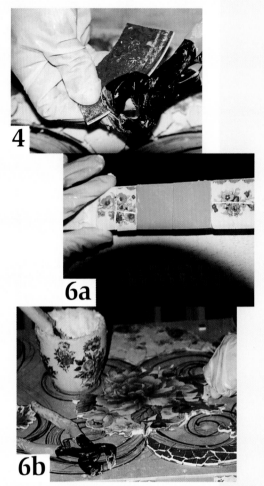

4

6a

6b

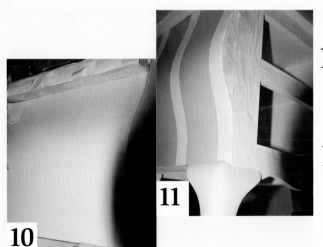

10

11

**10** Apply a base coat of ivory paint over areas that do not have mosaics, using 2" flat paintbrushes. Allow to dry.

**11** Mask off untiled sections of the night table for painted design. Cover tiled areas with paper and tape.

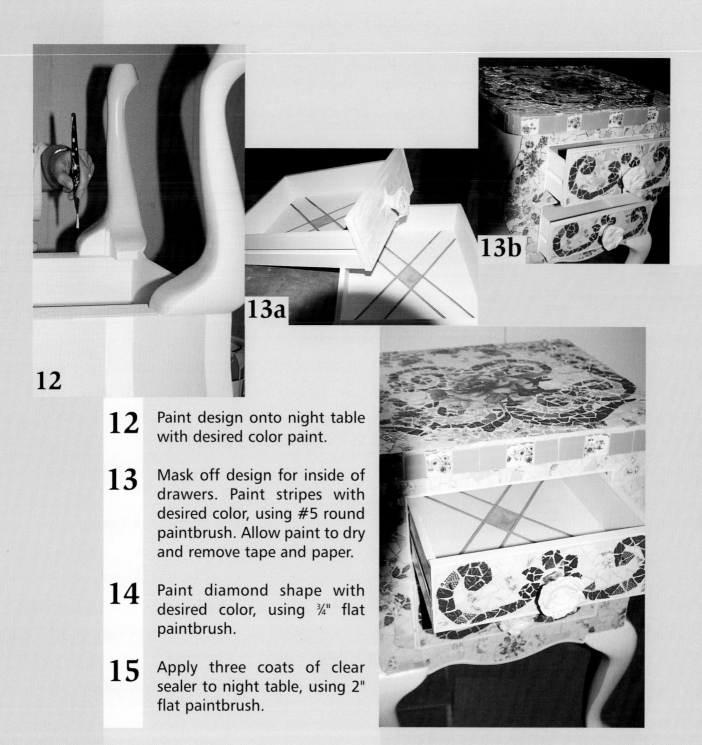

**12**    **12**   Paint design onto night table with desired color paint.

**13a**   **13b**

**13**   Mask off design for inside of drawers. Paint stripes with desired color, using #5 round paintbrush. Allow paint to dry and remove tape and paper.

**14**   Paint diamond shape with desired color, using ¾" flat paintbrush.

**15**   Apply three coats of clear sealer to night table, using 2" flat paintbrush.

TONY MACK Tony was born in 1956 in Los Angeles, California, one of six children. He has been heavily encouraged by his family in the arts and crafts since childhood.

Tony began painting in high school as well as apprenticing for a series of artists—washing their brushes and stretching their canvases.

Early in his career he was hired to paint individual portraits of a family in Northern California, which took several years to complete. He was encouraged by his studio mate to show his paintings, and found success. However, feeling that he did not fit into the "gallery scene," he then returned to his studio and decided to work three-dimensionally. He produced a line of furniture and came to the realization that his studio was a storefront on a major thoroughfare, so he opened a furniture store, creating furniture the way he thought that it should look. Currently, he incorporates all that he loves stylistically into his work, including découpage.

Découpage, the art of applying paper with an adhesive in a decorative fashion, was coined in France sometime in the 1700s. The sources of inspiration for Tony's découpage are peeling billboards, old show signs, advertising images, old stained newspapers, trading stamps, and theater leaflets. Tony says that "vintage wallpaper and an assortment of love letters have a beauty that cannot be matched."

**Upper:** Miscellaneous material sources for découpage

**Upper left:** Découpaged and painted chest and side table
**Upper right:** Découpaged and painted chest of drawers
**Left:** Credenza découpaged with maps

# DÉCOUPAGED CHEST

## Materials & Supplies

Assorted papers
Latex paint: porch or floor
Razor blades
Sandpaper: 80 grit
Scissors
Vintage chest of drawers: prepped*
Water-based varnish: satin
Wood glue: yellow
Paintbrushes: 1½"; 2"; 3"

*Prepped as applicable. See page 57.

DO'S AND DON'TS IN SELECTING PAPER FOR DÉCOUPAGE:

• Do not use glossy paper, it slips, slides, and curls (Including postcards)
• Do not use pre-1940s red ink, it tends to run
• Use color copies or laser-printed images (color copies have intensified color and are colorfast)
• Allow the paper to determine how to be used

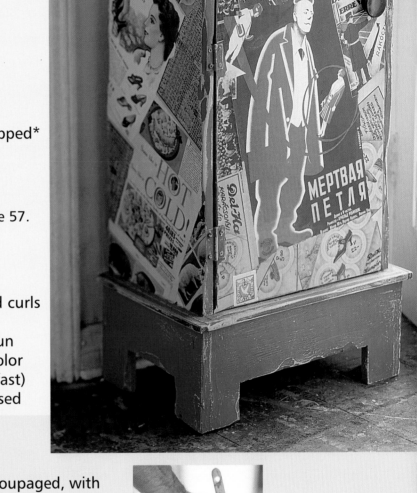

1 Paint any trim areas that will not be découpaged, with latex paint, using 1½" paintbrush. Allow to dry. Repeat with second coat.

2 Lightly sand paint to give an aged or distressed appearance.

3 Cut paper as desired for découpage.

1

**4** Apply layer of wood glue onto top surface of chest (in a space no larger than one square foot), using 2" paintbrush.

**5** Position paper on glue. Apply a layer of glue on paper. Note: If a smooth surface is desired, wait 10–15 minutes for glue to set up before applying second layer of glue.

**6** Continue applying glue and paper onto chest, completing one section at a time. Note: An area may be allowed to dry, then added onto later. Allow glue to dry 24 hours or until completely dry.

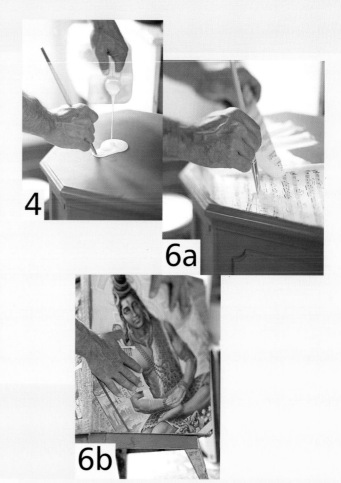

4

6a

6b

6c

**7** Sand the surface and edges, wearing through some of the découpaged paper. Go slowly, surveying the overall appearance. Gently remove all dust.

**8** Apply three coats of varnish, using 3" paintbrush. Allow varnish to dry between coats.

LYNN BONGE Lynn has been painting for approximately twenty years, and since the mid-nineties, she has been drawn to painting wonderful designs on furniture, or what she refers to as "functional art."

She tries to achieve a soft "smooshy" feel on her furniture and is especially fond of the Country European look, which she feels is more sophisticated than the American Country. She likes using common everyday things to decorate her furniture line—fruits, vegetables, flowers, and even animals. Her company, Camden Field—named after her youngest granddaughter—brought "Le Chanticleer," the rooster, to the marketplace over two years ago. This was long before anyone else was painting roosters on furniture. She is told that he is still one of the best looking roosters around.

Lynn is self-taught as a painter and understands that painting is a gift from God, so He is the one who should get the honor.

**Center:** Painted rooster detail
**Right:** "Le Coq" buffet server in black and red

**Upper left:** "Michaud Grapes" French armoire
**Upper right:** "Les Fleurs de Georgette" sleigh bed
**Lower right:** "Fruit in Delft" sideboard

## Materials & Supplies

Acrylic latex paint: ivory
Acrylic paints: black; dk.
   green; lt. green; nutmeg;
   red; raw sienna; straw;
   raw umber; antique white
Acrylic sealer: satin
Furniture: prepped*
General purpose spray cleaner
Graphite paper
Paintbrushes: #8 filbert; 1" flat;
   #40 liner
Water-based varnish

*Prepped as applicable. See page 57.

# PAINTED APPLES

The artist is teaching her painting technique and no project is shown.

1   Apply latex paint to table, using flat paintbrush. Allow to dry. Enlarge pattern on page 115 to desired size. Place graphite paper face down onto table. Place pattern onto graphite paper and trace design.

2   Wash straw paint over all leaves and apples with long smooth strokes, using filbert paintbrush. Allow to dry. Note: All paint should be diluted with water in a 1:1 ratio.

3   Wash nest with raw sienna paint. Wash tree branches with nutmeg paint, using narrow side of paintbrush. Allow to dry.

**4**

**5–6**

**7**

**4** Wash leaves with lt. green paint.

**5** Apply more depth of color to apples and caterpillar with straw paint. Allow to dry.

**6** Wash blush onto apples with red paint.

**7** Paint underside of leaves with dk. green paint. Paint eggs with antique white paint.

**8** Add a deeper tone to apples with red paint.

**9** Wash over "shaded" area of nest with a blend of nutmeg and raw umber paints. Clean brush, and using more water than paint, add speckles onto eggs.

**10** Add legs and antennae to caterpillar with black paint, using liner brush. Shade caterpillar with raw sienna paint. Allow to dry.

**8**

**9–10**

**11** Wash underside of branches, apples, and leaves with raw umber paint to give depth, using filbert paintbrush. Allow to dry.

**12** Add veins to leaves with antique white paint, using liner paintbrush. Allow to dry.

**13** Add a little red to leaves as reflection from apples with red paint, using filbert paintbrush. Wash raw sienna, red, and lt. green paints around outside edges.

**14** Highlight design with a wash of mostly water and antique white paint.

**15** Apply three coats of varnish. Allow varnish to dry between coats.

**11**

**12–13**

**14**

PATTERN

**ROBYN FILLIMAN** Robyn has drawn since she can remember, art is a primary element in her life. She lives with her husband David and her daughter Lillian. She has a degree in Fine Arts from Southeastern Massachusetts University where she learned how to paint and how to make ceramics, along with a little steel work. In the past, she earned a living by making pottery and roughly built painted furniture. In the last five years, she and Dave have been operating a small wholesale business. Dave builds refined accent pieces such as frames, boxes, tables, and lamps; and Robyn decorates them.

In the beginning of the business, Robyn would paint each image onto the furniture. Because of the difficulty of keeping the painting quality consistent, she started experimenting with a "low pressure" laminate process using colored reproductions of her original artwork on paper. She coats the laminated color copy with a water-based urethane to seal it onto the wood.

**Upper:** "happy couple" mantle clock and "the gardeners" jewelry box

**Upper:** "house in the hills" table lamp, "houses in the hills" computer desk, and "my life with pets" trunk
**Right (clockwise):** "tree people" mirror frame, "purple jacket" CD cabinet, "in the woods" mirror frame, jewelry box, and "tea party" accent table

117

# ARTWORK DÉCOUPAGE

## Materials & Supplies

Air pen
Brayer
Bristle paper (11" x 17")
Casine tube paints: assorted
     colors
Gesso: black
Paintbrush: 2" flat; assorted sizes
Polyurethane
Pencil
Ruler
Scissors
Wood furniture: prepped*

*Prepped as applicable. See page 57.

2a

1 Sketch out design on bristle paper. Paint design with casine tube paints, using desired paintbrushes. Colorcopy design to desired dimensions. Note: Existing artwork could be colorcopied if desired.

2 Cut out design. Lightly apply coat of polyurethane to back of design, using flat paintbrush. Allow to dry. Repeat for front of design. Allow to dry.

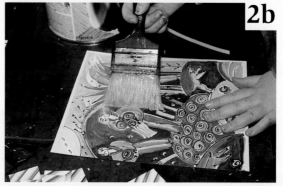

2b

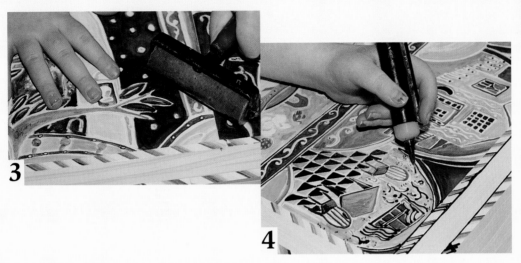

3 Apply polyurethane to back of design and to wood surface where art will be applied. Immediately place design onto surface and roll smooth, using brayer. Allow to dry. Note: Polyurethane will set up in seconds, so you will have limited working time.

4 Add decorative black line along edge of paper (hides edges) and elsewhere as desired, using air pen and black gesso. Note: An air pen will give a cleaner line and adds texture to the surface.

**Right:** Detail of "purple jacket" artwork

**Upper:** Vanity and mirror, mixed media
**Lower:** Detail of painted wallpaper trimming on vanity drawer

The Rosenberg Women: Elaine Rosenberg, Susan Wechsler, and Anita Rosenberg

**ELAINE ROSENBERG** Elaine (mother of Anita and Susan) graduated in Interior Design from Ohio State University. Later, she was the proprietress of a home accessory shop. She would shop in the United States and Europe for collections for her store. With her children grown, she continues to travel and acquires ideas as well as materials to use in her creations. She finds Spain inspirational because of the fabulous tiles; and everything about Morocco gives her ideas. The buildings there are covered with mosaics in

wonderful bright geometric patterns. She photographs everything of interest and uses it for reference at a later date.

Elaine's work is purely for her own pleasure and it is not for sale. She finds many of her furniture pieces at flea markets, unfinished furniture stores, and antique shops. She feels that collecting is a part of each project.

**Upper left:** Detail of dresser front with painted wooden scroll and medallion trims
**Lower left:** Side view of dresser, mixed media including wallpaper, and painted
**Right:** Front view of dresser

**Left:** Side view of buffet, art glass and painted
**Lower:** Front view of buffet

SUSAN WECHSLER Growing up among artists had some great life lessons for Susan. At the age of eighteen, she accepted an opportunity to paint an abstract design on a billboard in down-town Cincinnati where she grew up. She was presented "the key to the city" from then mayor, Jerry Springer.

Susan received a Bachelor of Fine Arts degree in sculpture, and a Master of Fine Arts degree in theater design from NYU. After designing for Off-Broadway theatre in New York City and "B" movies in Hollywood, she married and moved to San Francisco to design clothing for Espirit.

Following a move back to Cincinnati with her hus-band, David, and sons, Zachary and Andrew, Susan was looking for a creative outlet. She began by painting every wall, piece of furniture, and accessory in their home. Friends started requesting that she paint a wall or a dress-er, and before she knew it a "cottage" business had begun.

Susan primarily designs children's rooms—due to her theatrical background. She finds that her whimsical, fanciful, and colorful style is well suited to children.

**Left:** Zachary and Andrew, posing with resin pig designed and painted by Susan for Cincinnati's Big Pig Gig

**Upper left:** Stenciled china cabinet
**Upper right:** Stenciled powder room wall
**Right:** Painted buffet with découpaged flowers

# BABY'S MEMORY BOX

## Materials & Supplies

Acrylic paints: soft white; assorted colors
Crackle medium
Découpage medium
Dry rag
Masking tape: ¾"
Paintbrushes: 1" flat; 2" flat
Photocopy of poem
Polycrylic varnish: clear semi-gloss
Sandpaper
Wooden box with lid: prepped*

*Prepped as applicable. See page 57.

**2a**

**2b**

**1** Base coat box with soft white paint, using 2" flat paintbrush.

**2** Place tape at ¾" intervals across box lid. Paint stripes with three alternating colors between tape strips, using 1" paintbrush. Note: While paint is still wet, wipe off any excess paint. Allow to dry and remove tape. Lightly sand.

**3a**

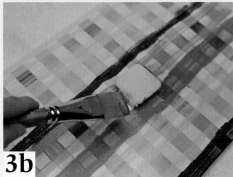

**3b**

**3** Place tape in opposite direction at uneven intervals to create plaid stripes. Paint five alternating colors between tape strips. Allow to dry and remove tape.

**4** Place tape around upper ⅓ of box bottom to create stripes. Apply crackle medium between taped areas, using 2" paintbrush. Allow to dry.

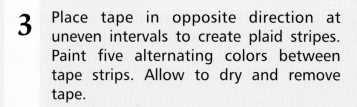

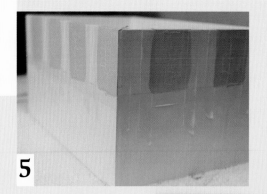

**5**

**5** Apply paint over crackle. Allow to dry and remove tape.

**6** Repeat Steps 4–5 with second color of paint.

**7** Paint bottom ⅔ of box. Allow to dry.

**6**

**7**

**8** Paint dots on box. Paint baby's name and birth date on bottom ⅔ of box. Allow to dry.

**9** Apply varnish to box and lid. Allow to dry.

**10** Découpage photocopy of poem to inside bottom of lid. Optional: Glue decorative trim around outside edge of poem for frame.

8–9

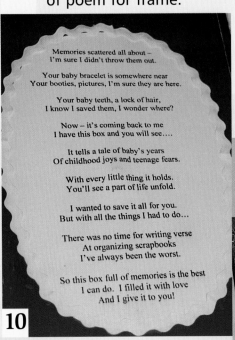

> Memories scattered all about –
> I'm sure I didn't throw them out.
>
> Your baby bracelet is somewhere near
> Your booties, pictures, I'm sure they are here.
>
> Your baby teeth, a lock of hair,
> I know I saved them, I wonder where?
>
> Now – it's coming back to me
> I have this box and you will see....
>
> It tells a tale of baby's years
> Of childhood joys and teenage fears.
>
> With every little thing it holds.
> You'll see a part of life unfold.
>
> I wanted to save it all for you.
> But with all the things I had to do...
>
> There was no time for writing verse
> At organizing scrapbooks
> I've always been the worst.
>
> So this box full of memories is the best
> I can do. I filled it with love
> And I give it to you!

10

**Lower right:** Painted frames and Baby's Memory Box

## ABOUT THE ARTIST

Anita Rosenberg is an artist and filmmaker with her own unique vision of the world around her. A self-professed adventurer and world traveler, Anita finds her biggest inspiration from trips throughout the United States as well as abroad. Whether she creates her "Tuscan Farmhouse" and "Italy" collections after a trip to Portofino on the Italian Riviera or her "Leopard" and "Bamboo" designs after an expedition to Hong Kong and Bali, Anita's work is always fresh and fun.

Her art education began at the Cincinnati Art Museum while she was still in High School. After winning many awards for her photography and sculpture, Anita embarked on her childhood dream of art school. She continued her love of welding metal sculpture at the San Francisco Art Institute, receiving a Bachelor of Fine Arts degree. While experiencing the free-spirited independent film scene with teacher and mentor, George Kuchar, Anita added filmmaking to her multi-media focus.

"Every young artist must have the New York experience," so with that in mind, Anita moved to New York City to attend the prestigious NYU Graduate Film School. Along with fellow classmate, Spike Lee, Anita submerged herself in filmmaking. She found it the ultimate "art form," encompassing sound, visuals, and story. Her thesis film, *Bachelorette Pad,* was the story of Candy Stone, a swinging single bachelorette. It had animated Barbie dolls that came to life. With an MFA in directing in her hand, she moved out West to pursue her film career in the movie capital of the world, Los Angeles.

After thirteen years and two films under her belt, *Modern Girls* and the cult classic *Assault of the Killer Bimbos,* Anita longed for more immediate artistic satisfaction. While under preproduction for *The Legend of the Swedish Bikini Team* or *Viking Girls on Spring Break,* she began her own company hand-painting accessories. When the movie failed to move forward, Anita focused on her business and the Anita Rosenberg Studio was born.

Wanting to be the "Ralph Lauren" of the funky hand-painted world, she created a large collection of tables, lamps, candlesticks, trays, and frames whose purpose was to mix-and-match. Six years later, and with customers all over the globe, Anita is proud to share with you some of her own inspirations and self-invented techniques so that you, too, might discover the joy of painting your own furniture.

Anita's first collectors were her movieland friends and colleagues, George Clooney, Arnold Schwarzenegger, Tom Cruise and Nicole Kidman, John Travolta and Kelly Preston, Spike Lee, Tom Hanks, Jennifer Love Hewitt, Elizabeth Taylor, and Jennifer Aniston. Her work can also be seen on television shows, *Friends, Suddenly Susan, Melrose Place, Seinfeld, The Practice, Good Morning America,* and *Sabrina the Teenage Witch.*

# ACKNOWLEDGMENTS

My deepest thanks and appreciation to my magnificent studio staff of painters, Anastasiya Kaunator and Zigrida Kaunator. I want to thank Christopher Wheeler who has been my supportive business associate and good friend. Also, thank you to my inspirational high school art teacher Dorothy Dobbins, who calls me one of her "17 angels." Thank you to my power tool guru, Al Cornett, who opened my eyes to the amazing world of machinery. And a final super-duper thank you to my loving and supportive family who has believed in me and supported me throughout my artistic career. Even though I am not quite ready to mention you in my *People Magazine* article yet, I want to thank you dearly in my first book, Marvin, Elaine, Susan, David, Barry, David W., Gina, Zachary, Drew, Max, and baby Oliver.

# GALLERY ARTISTS' INFORMATION

Lynn Bonge (Camden Fields)
The Michauds
140 Paris Glen Way
Greenville, SC 29609

Rebecca Dennis and Paula Funt
(Mosaicwares)
160 Tycos drive
Toronto, Canada m6b 1w8
Phone: (416) 787-5526
Fax: (416) 787-5424
email: mosaicwares@look.ca
Website: www.mosaicwares.com

Robyn Filliman
Phone: (603) 239-7425
email: rfilliman@aol.com

Tony Mack
7950 W. Third Street
Los Angeles, CA 90048
Phone: (323) 655-5711

Anita Rosenberg
1010 Fernando Rd.
Los Angeles, CA 90065
Phone: (323) 227-8180
Fax (323) 227-8182
email: arstudio@aol.com
Website: www.anitarosenberg.com

Susan Wechsler
email: swechsler@cinci.rr.com

# METRIC CONVERSION CHART

cm—Centimetres
Inches to Centimetres

| inches | cm | inches | cm |
|--------|------|--------|------|
| ⅛ | 0.3 | 13 | 33.0 |
| ¼ | 0.6 | 14 | 35.6 |
| ½ | 1.3 | 15 | 38.1 |
| ⅝ | 1.6 | 16 | 40.6 |
| ¾ | 1.9 | 17 | 43.2 |
| ⅞ | 2.2 | 18 | 45.7 |
| 1 | 3.2 | 19 | 48.3 |
| 1¼ | 3.2 | 20 | 50.8 |
| 1½ | 3.8 | 21 | 53.3 |
| 1¾ | 4.4 | 22 | 55.9 |
| 2 | 5.1 | 23 | 58.4 |
| 2½ | 6.4 | 24 | 61.0 |
| 3 | 7.6 | 25 | 63.5 |
| 3½ | 8.9 | 26 | 66.0 |
| 4 | 10.2 | 27 | 68.6 |
| 4½ | 11.4 | 28 | 71.1 |
| 5 | 12.7 | 29 | 73.7 |
| 6 | 15.2 | 30 | 76.2 |
| 7 | 17.8 | 31 | 78.7 |
| 8 | 20.3 | 32 | 80.2 |
| 9 | 22.9 | 33 | 83.8 |
| 10 | 25.4 | 34 | 86.4 |
| 11 | 27.9 | 35 | 88.9 |
| 12 | 30.5 | 36 | 91.4 |

# RECOMMENDED READING

*Junk Chic*–Kathryn Elliott

*Feng Shui Chic*–Sharon Stasney

*Tricia Guild in Town: Contemporary Design for Urban Living*–Tricia Guild

*Tricia Guild on Color*–Tricia Guild

*Tricia Guild's Country Color*–Tricia Guild

*The Western Guide to Feng Shui: Creating Balance, Harmony, and Prosperity in Your Environment*–Terah Kathryn Collins

*American Junk: How to Hunt for, Haggle Over, Rescue, and Transform America's Forgotten Treasures*–Mary Randolph Carter

*Garden Junk*–Mary Randolph Carter

# RESOURCES

Craft Wholesalers
Wholesale craft paints to the trade
Phone: (800) 666-5858

Frank's
Multiple locations in the midwest

Nova Color
Bulk paint for artists
Phone: (310) 204-6900
Los Angeles, CA

Michael's
Nationwide locations

Pearl
World's Largest Art & Craft Discount Center
Locations: FL, GA, IL, MA, NJ, NY, PA, VA
Phone for catalogue:
(800) 451-pearl

The Art Store
Multiple locations in Los Angeles, CA

# INDEX